Governor

Julie Murray

Abdo
MY GOVERNMENT
Kids

abdopublishing.com

Published by Abdo Kids, a division of ABDO, P.O. Box 398166, Minneapolis, Minnesota 55439.
Copyright © 2018 by Abdo Consulting Group, Inc. International copyrights reserved in all countries.
No part of this book may be reproduced in any form without written permission from the publisher.
Abdo Kids Junior™ is a trademark and logo of Abdo Kids.

Printed in the United States of America, North Mankato, Minnesota.

102017

012018

THIS BOOK CONTAINS
RECYCLED MATERIALS

Photo Credits: AP Images, Glow Images, iStock, Shutterstock, USAF,
©Dannel Malloy p.22/CC-BY-2.0, ©Michael Vadon p.22/CC-BY-SA-4.0

Production Contributors: Teddy Borth, Jennie Forsberg, Grace Hansen

Design Contributors: Christina Doffing, Candice Keimig, Dorothy Toth

Publisher's Cataloging in Publication Data

Names: Murray, Julie, author.

Title: Governor / by Julie Murray.

Description: Minneapolis, Minnesota : Abdo Kids, 2018. | Series: My government |
    Includes glossary, index and online resource (page 24).

Identifiers: LCCN 2017942862 | ISBN 9781532103971 (lib.bdg.) | ISBN 9781532105098 (ebook) |
    ISBN 9781532105654 (Read-to-me ebook)

Subjects: LCSH: Governors--United States--Juvenile literature.

Classification: DDC 352.232130973--dc23

LC record available at https://lccn.loc.gov/2017942862

Table of Contents

Governor

Each state has one. He or she is voted in.

They have a big job to do.

They help run their state.

They can sign **bills**. They make sure a new law is followed.

They work on a **budget**. They choose how to spend it.

They go to city events.

They make speeches.

They make sure people are safe.

16

17

They live in a **special** house.

Who is your governor?

What is the Governor's Job?

decide how money
is spent

give speeches

lead a state

sign new laws

Glossary

bill
an idea for a new state law that must be passed by a governor.

budget
a plan for how much money will be spent in a certain amount of time.

special
having a certain purpose. Most states have a special house for their governor to live in.

Index

Abdo Kids
ONLINE
FREE! ONLINE MULTIMEDIA RESOURCES

Visit **abdokids.com** and use this code to access crafts, games, videos, and more!

Abdo Kids Code:
MGK3971